I0540730

AM I THE A**HOLE?

Your Words and Actions Matter

Dana Baker

Terra Publishing

Tampa, FL

Terra Publishing, Tampa FL

Hardcover ISBN: 978-0-9661066-9-5

Paperback ISBN: 978-1-962424-06-6

E-book ISBN: 978-1-962424-07-3

Library of Congress Control Number: 2025904141

Cover Design: Taherul Khan and Dana Baker

In some cases, names have been changed to protect privacy.

DISCLAIMER

This book is designed to provide information about the subject matter covered. It is sold with the understanding that the publisher and author are not engaged in rendering any psychological and medical advice or services. If expert assistance is desired or required, the services of a competent professional should be sought.

The purpose of this book is to share and encourage. The publisher and author shall have neither liability nor responsibility to any person or entity with respect to any loss or damage caused or alleged to be caused directly or indirectly by the information contained in this book.

DEDICATION

For those who have been mistreated or who have
mistreated others.

CONTENTS

PREFACE

One day, rather abruptly, my three-year friendship with Maggie came to an end. I thought it was a good friendship, based on our common interest in swimming. After attempting to contact her three times over the course of a month, I concluded that something went wrong. I'm 90% sure why she ended the friendship, and I didn't want to admit it or accept it at first.

Something that bothered her in the past resurfaced and she no longer wanted to deal with me. I crossed a line, and I was disposed of with no warning. I did a lot of soul searching and I believe I was an a**hole. That's a difficult realization because I pride myself on being a good friend to everyone.

What did I do to offend her? I mentioned the need for a few kayakers for our upcoming five-mile swim because we would have swimmers at varying speeds. She said, "I'm tired of you always (this was the fourth time in three years) mentioning that you and Carla need a different kayaker." She got upset because it drew attention to her slower pace. If I didn't say anything, it could pose safety issues and practical problems for the upcoming swim we were planning.

I felt I needed to say something, but perhaps I didn't show enough compassion. The topic we were discussing was a delicate subject matter for her, and can be a little abrasive at times.

What I've learned is that it's more important to be gentle than direct. Kindness. Even if something is true and necessary to say, you must present it tactfully.

After a few months, I concluded that the friendship was enjoyable while it lasted and now, she's better off without me and I'm better off without her. To soften the blow of the loss of Maggie, I called to mind the few times I witnessed her discarding certain people in her life and on a few occasions, she switched emotions instantly. If she easily dropped me without explanation, what type of friend was that?

Maybe there were more reasons Maggie dropped me, but she didn't indicate anything. I thought about how I treated or mistreated Maggie. Then I considered, "In what other situations, with other people, was I obnoxious?"

This is what we'll explore in this book – the importance of self-awareness, considering others' perspectives, admitting when you've offended someone, and making changes that demonstrate kindness and compassion.

INTRODUCTION

I'm not proud of my a**holish moments. They cause harm. I've lost friends and have alienated people. My character is generally good, but I have my moments. In some ways, I'm a recovering a**hole. I'm somewhat reformed, but not completely cured.

I'm still working on not reacting impulsively when I'm threatened. Why is it that when I'm provoked, I sometimes lash out? Emotional immaturity, habit, prior wounding? Why do I sometimes trigger others? Jealousy, arrogance, and insecurity come to mind.

I suspect my "inner child" is screaming out in pain or that I feel threatened. I end up feeling like some of my actions and reactions are an attempt to establish power. Perhaps I'm compensating for feeling ignored or unimportant.

We can change our words and behaviors, but

we'll make mistakes if we don't do the inner work needed to improve. I'm still doing the inner work.

This book is an invitation to journey to the uncomfortable parts of yourself. It's been a therapy of sorts for me. I'm still unraveling the immaturity, wretchedness, and weak parts of myself that seem incongruent with my outwardly respectable demeanor. I accept and understand that dichotomy about myself, but I don't like it, and I don't want to spend much time dwelling on it.

But we must dwell. We must enter the part of ourselves that's closed or buried. The only way to solve a problem is to identify the problem. For maximum psychological and emotional growth, every stone must be unearthed. Otherwise, we feel something is slightly off. We feel inauthentic and incomplete.

Have you ever stopped to think that maybe you're a jerk sometimes, to some people? Why is it that when we hear our friends talk about their divorce or relationship problems that the other person wronged them? They think the other person is at fault. How come it's seldom our friend?

In Am I the A**hole? (AITA), you'll determine if you're the culprit in some of your interactions or relationships. AITA shows you where you might have gone wrong, what to do if you've been an a**hole, and how to stop your distasteful ways. In this one-of-a-kind book, you'll quietly examine yourself.

Many people are unaware when they say or do something that's obnoxious. AITA will show you what to look for and how to mend your ways. You can't afford to neglect behavior that can ultimately cost you your job and relationships.

I hope you'll contemplate whether you've been an a**hole. It's time to examine ourselves and put an end to being an a**hole. This book is for anyone who's ever lost friendships, for those who wish to examine a darker side of themselves, and for those who want to guard against being an a**hole. We're not as great and as pure as we think we are.

If you continue being an a**hole, it may cost you your job, career, relationships, or marriage. Take comfort in knowing we've all been an a**hole to someone at some point. The key is to become aware of it and take ownership.

The passage of time has provided healing for me. I'm grateful to those who've dumped me or called me out on my insensitive words and lack of compassion. They brought a new awareness to my life. If I've offended someone, I silently ask for their forgiveness. For those who've been cruel to me, I forgive them. I admit that forgiveness of a few select people is still ongoing.

This book would not be possible without several wake-up calls, including the recent and shocking end of my friendship with Maggie. After doing a lot of introspection, I wasn't surprised about the unwanted turn of events.

Friendships come and go. The endings are sad. Some endings aren't chosen, and some relationships run their course. The seasons change and so do we. Transformations are life-enhancing, and the good news is that everything is subject to change. Everything is in transition. We muddle our way through the process of those bittersweet transitions, and we must adopt a new attitude and direction if we are forlorn or downtrodden. It's time to tackle taboo topics.

PART I - THE WHO, WHAT AND WHY OF BEING AN A**HOLE

1 WHAT IS AN A**HOLE?

What exactly is an a**hole? Labeling someone an asshole involves perception and opinion and is the result of an interpreted experience. It's a real experience in which meaning is assigned.

Am I an A**hole?

How do you know if you're an a**hole? Many forums on Redditt and YouTube address this issue. If you're unsure, one way is to consult social media, but be aware, it's filled with opinions. That's ok. This book is filled with opinions.

Most of us would agree that an a**hole is a mean, confrontational, contemptible person. We attribute the term to a personality. But sometimes, people behave in a single episode that we deem unnerving. Most of us are a**holes occasionally.

Someone can be called an a**hole after a one-time event, or an a**hole can be someone with repulsive character traits. I would call the driver of a pickup truck who intentionally speeds into a crowd with the intent to kill, an a**hole. Any act of intentional, malicious homicide warrants using the term a**hole. Someone who inflicts, allows, or causes harm to others: a**hole.

Maybe someone isn't a full-blown a**hole, but rather appalling, condescending, stubborn, unyielding, secretive, stuck-up, snobby, smug, egotistical, irrational, unreasonable, irritating, irate, abrasive, repulsive, selfish, pretentious, phony, or antagonistic. Maybe they're a miscreant, rascal, or scalawag.

Terminology

Although you'll see the word asshole (or a**hole) over a hundred times in this book, I use it freely because this is the topic of the book. In my everyday life, I use the word sparingly and prefer to use another word in its place.

"Asshole" is a powerful, universally known word, and somewhat vulgar. Saying the word "asshole" can be uncomfortable and feels like a bold proclamation. I'd like to soften the intensity and use synonyms throughout this book including some of the above words, especially "unkind" and "twit."

Other words that come to mind in describing an a**hole: butthole, ass, jackass, a-hole, ass hat, AH, ass wipe, obstinate, obnoxious, annoying, arrogant, incorrigible, idiot, fool, aggravator, agitator, abusive, narcissist, liar, manipulator, explosive, exploitive, exploitative, egregious, deceptive, despicable, deplorable, opportunist, schmuck, jerk, pompous, proud, unpleasant, disagreeable, abhorrent, know-it-all, superior, subversive, sinister, snake, thief, criminal, psychopath, sociopath.

I sometimes pronounce the title of this book in public by saying, Am I the Asteriskhole? I occasionally use "ass" or another word on the occasions I feel warranted referring to someone as an asshole. You'll see me use a**hole, assholish, and assholeness.

Pardon me if you don't like the word or feel it's overused here, but we must fully discuss this topic if we want to make progress in decreasing the poor human treatment that assholeness incites.

Perspective and Meaning

Let's say I have a good friend visiting for a few days and she decides to go on a long walk. I perform a favor by washing her car in my driveway. I feel happy and helpful because the dirty car is now clean, and my visitor has had a busy week.

My visitor returns and says, "Thanks for washing my car, but I was going to take it to the car wash next week. You didn't have to wash it." She might be insulted and think of me as controlling and judgmental. Two completely different perspectives regarding a car being washed!

If you're driving on the highway and someone pulls into your lane, cutting you off, risking an accident, you might think the person is a jerk. Someone else might think the driver was incompetent and someone else might think the person had an emergency.

Different reactions follow different thoughts. One driver might blast his horn, yell, or make a gesture at the erratic driver. Another might be understanding and do nothing, thinking "oh well," and continue driving safely. As you'll see, one behavior can trigger others, and this will be a topic of discussion in AITA.

We make up stories and assign meaning to various occurrences. For most of my life, I've noticed conversations where people blame another person.

"I wasn't promoted. Someone else got the job and didn't deserve it."

"I was treated poorly at the doctor's office."

"I should have been voted Most Valuable Player on my soccer team."

"My teacher gave me a B."

There's always more to a story, and the storyteller's imagination and interpretation can construct many possibilities. It's common to hear our friends' stories about how they were mistreated. You seldom hear them admit they did a foolish thing or mistreated another.

Many of my friends have been on the receiving end of injustice. How come they rarely share how they acted unreasonably? They got divorced because their spouse mistreated them, had an affair, or didn't keep the vows as promised.

Hours and hours of conversations include how and why someone else was inconsiderate, selfish, narcissistic, or mean. Someone else was disrespectful or manipulative.

Maybe Yes, Maybe No

You may be an a**hole, or maybe not. If you think you are, make amends. If you think someone else is, take precautions.

I'm an a**hole. Sometimes. Usually not on purpose. If I've been an ass, it's probably because I've been provoked to the point of retaliation. I feel the need to protect myself, my reputation, character, or whatever it is I'm trying to preserve. On occasion, I lie and compromise my morals when I'm cornered by a difficult person. If I'm feeling weak or insecure, I'm at risk of lying.

Other times, I'm out of line. I might be too nosy and meddlesome. I might gossip or speak unkindly about someone. Almost always, it's unintentional. Still, some of my words and actions qualify for being an a**hole.

Our words, actions, thoughts of others, and treatment of others matter. When we call people derogatory names, we reduce them to one component of their humanity. It causes psychological and spiritual injury to both of us.

Mistaken for an A**hole

I can think of three occasions when I've been mistaken for being an a**hole. We must remember that the accuser's perception influences whether someone is an a**hole.

When I don't say hello to someone who recognizes me and who I should recognize, I can be accused of being rude. I hate this situation! I'm grateful when someone points out that I didn't say anything or ignored them.

This happens if I haven't seen someone in a long time and their appearance is different. Maybe they've aged, gained weight, lost weight, or have a different hair style or color. Maybe I only see them at work in a uniform or in a certain setting and then when I see them in a completely different environment, they're dressed differently.

In high school, I was shy and quiet, and a teacher said I seemed hostile. This happened in a part-time job as well when I was 17. I have a serious facial expression that is sometimes misinterpreted.

One time in my early thirties, a few of the neighborhood women were planning a mom's night out. I received a call from someone about the details. I don't remember what was said during the conversation, but I recall that we were both assertive and decisive women. She felt that I was harsh and not interested in the outing. She was right. I remember the phone call being unpleasant, and I can't remember why I might have said something offensive. I never did go out with the group on that mom's night out.

Communicating with my female friends was different from talking with my male friends. Women preferred more politeness, and less bluntness and honesty, whereas with men I was able to be direct.

There are times you might be mistaken for being an a**hole. There's not a lot you can do about it. People usually hold firmly to their perceptions and beliefs.

Narcissism

Narcissism is on the rise. The word is used frequently, and it seems narcissists are born every day.

The truth is that narcissists aren't born, they're made. Narcissism is mostly a learned response, and part of one's development as a coping mechanism or adaptation because of one's environment. There are personality disorders that include narcissism as a component, but for the most part narcissists are made every day, not born every day.

I conducted research beginning in 2016 when I experienced harm from narcissists. I learned that I was a codependent. I was, and still am, a people-pleaser and a peacemaker. I read several books and watched hours of videos for over a year as I tried to unravel my frustration and confusion.

The following authors and experts helped me, along with many YouTube channels (indicated in parentheses):

- Dr. Ramani Durvasula (DoctorRamani)
- Dr. Sam Vaknin (Prof. Sam Vaknin)
- Dr. Ross Rosenberg (Ross Rosenberg)
- Dr. Meredith Resnick
- Dr. Linda Martinez-Lewi
- Melanie Tonia Evans (Melanie Tonia Evans)
- Lisa Romano (Lisa A. Romano)
- Christopher Kumaran (Narc Survivor)
- Quinn Holliday (Assc Podcast)
- H.G. Tudor (Knowing the Narcissist: Ultra)

- Kevin McKee (The Royal We)
- (The Little Shaman)
- Dr. Les Carter (Surviving Narcissism).

I produced a twenty-minute episode on my former podcast program in which I talked about what to do if you married a narcissist, techniques to try in dealing with a narcissist, and how to transform yourself from being a codependent victim. I offered hope for the future.

The narcissist can bring out the worst in you, cause emotional trauma or depression, and cause chaos. Narcissistic Personality Disorder (NPD) is recognized in the Diagnostic and Statistical Manual (DSM) of Mental Disorders Vol. 5 as a personality disorder. There's a lot of speculation whether narcissism is a mental illness, behavioral disorder, or personality disorder.

Labels and diagnoses of "borderline" personality disorders are often given to narcissists. It can be a messy web to untangle. The key is in assessing what you're dealing with.

After spending a few years studying narcissism and being a victim of narcissism, a bomb was dropped on me one day.

As my husband pulled out a small notebook, he proclaimed, "Oh yeah, you're a narcissist. I made a lot of notes, but I'm not ready to share them with you yet." I was stung and managed to reply, "O.K. I hope you'll share them one day when you're ready."

Thirty days later, he shared his notes. I understood his perspective, but I was startled about some things. He pointed out that a few of my family members were narcissists, and it wasn't surprising that I adopted some traits and behaviors like other family members.

I asked for specifics from my husband and others close to me who thought I might have narcissistic tendencies. People close to me agreed that I wasn't a full-blown narcissist, but that I do sometimes feel overly important. They agreed that I have a lack of empathy about others' feelings on occasion, and that I can be arrogant and interruptive. I quickly got to work on some of the things they mentioned.

When I told one friend who's known me for over 25 years that my husband said I have narcissistic tendencies, she said, "You're the nicest narcissist I know." I got a kick out of that, knowing that there are mostly negatives associated with narcissism. She sees the good side of me, accepts me for who I am, and like other immediate family members, agreed that I have minor narcissistic tendencies. I began to view narcissism a little differently.

It makes sense that narcissists can have asshole tendencies. Here are some DSM-5 criteria for Narcissistic Personality Disorder (NPD): grandiosity, fantasies (of success, power, beauty, or ideal love), specialness, entitlement, exploitation, lack of empathy, envy, arrogance, and need for admiration.

Selfies and Selfishness

The root of narcissism is selfishness. Self-aggrandizement is attention to the self. Self-absorption is being immersed in your own self and is also referred to as being self-centered. The cultural landscape doesn't encourage humility.

Look no further than our "selfie" saturated world. What was the world like before "selfies?" Selfies are photos or pictures people take of themselves alone or with others. Selfies are thought to have originated in Australia in 2002 when someone took a picture of himself to document an injury. Nowadays, selfies are commonplace and almost an artform. They're fun and they help create memories.

Preoccupation with social media results in people taking several photos per day, paying more attention to their appearance than ever before. If selfies were around when I was in high school, I would have despised them. Selfies favor those who are confident and comfortable in an appearance-focused culture.

Selfies contribute to our narcissistic society. People like to post selfies publicly, not only to share information, but to brag or draw attention to themselves. Selfies emphasize the individual and are often staged to present a certain image.

People are extra careful to appear camera-ready so that they portray themselves in the most favorable manner. We weren't concerned with striking a pose throughout the day in the pre-selfie era and usually posed for pictures during selected moments or special occasions.

Some people go beyond presenting themselves to the best of their ability. They go to the extreme of enhancing or altering their appearance by injecting harmful toxic substances into their face and body. There's been an increase in cosmetic surgery in the last several years as many people clamor to look younger or what they perceive as better.

Americans spend over four hours a day on screen time. 10% of heavy users touch their phone 5,400 times a day and spend three hours a day on videos. Of course they will be bombarded with images that emphasize physical appearance. This feeds into narcissism, which can lead to a**hole tendencies.

What Does an Asshole Want?

An asshole wants what we all want but goes about it in a convoluted way. For starters, we want to be noticed, understood, respected and loved. We want to make a difference in this world. We're looking for solutions to our problems. Many of us want a pain-free, easy life.

The incorrigible one likely has deep wounds and acts out in distasteful ways. Trauma, wounds, and brokenness are often at the core of a chronic a**hole. This is why I have a hard time using the word asshole and labeling myself an asshole.

Some would argue that a**holes don't care. I don't agree with that. **At their foundation, no one wants to be an asshole because it ultimately drives people away, which is the very outcome the asshole doesn't want.** A**holes crave what the rest of us desire.

2 WHY ARE SOME PEOPLE A**HOLES?

We're impacted by numerous incidents throughout our lifetime. Our temperament and personality account for how we respond to what happens to us.

There are many reasons people act in harmful ways. For some, it's habitual. Others delight in a warped kind of satisfaction. Let's explore how a**holes are made and why some are prone to unfavorable treatment of others.

The Shaping of an Individual

Babies are born into different circumstances. They're born in various parts of the world into various families, different social classes, and different educational opportunities. Children are exposed to different experiences and activities. The shaping of a child depends on how they're raised and by whom. Children develop various temperaments and personality types.

Children may be encouraged in some areas of life, may be neglected, or feel unwanted or abandoned. Some children are given everything to the point they feel entitled. They may expect the most lavish and luxurious material goods. Everyone is taught different values, and some will adopt values even if they hadn't been taught them.

During various developmental stages, children need to have basic needs met and they learn attachment styles. They learn love and ways of behaving. They should be learning right from wrong, and parents or caregivers are responsible for guiding them with high standards of morals and values.

Children develop a sense of importance and preferences. They're learning about their place in the world and how they might fit in. Some children have a higher need for attention and admiration than others. A certain number become arrogant and bossy. Some are self-starters, and others need a lot of guidance. Children can behave in cooperative, competitive, conformant, and / or rebellious ways.

If a child doesn't feel loved and affirmed, he may feel lonely, insecure, and abandoned. This is when problems can emerge. Basically, there are numerous experiences that occur during a lifetime that shape a person.

Insecurity

I'm convinced that people are a**holes because they believe they lack something. They're angry that they've been robbed of a high level of nurturing and kindness. They lack love, affirmation, understanding, or validation. Maybe they felt abandoned or abused. Being an a**hole is a cry for love and attention. They may have been treated poorly by a difficult or abusive parent and now they act in ways that don't exhibit social and emotional maturity or thriving.

Feeling Superior

Sometimes when people feel insecure or inferior, they want to feel important or superior. This explains why some people say snide remarks. For example. Let's say your 28-year-old friend got divorced after a 10-year marriage to his high school girlfriend. Instead of saying "I'm sorry for you," you say "Oh well. Most teenage marriages don't last."

Your friend doesn't know this, but your motivation and feeling behind your comment was this: You're secretly jealous that the couple are attractive, outgoing, and charming – everything you wish you were. Making an unkind comment, and his demise, makes you feel superior.

Self-preservation

Self-preservation and protection explain why some people do certain things. If you feel obliged to guard your territory, you may resort to rude, illegal, or extreme actions if you feel threatened or fear intruders. If you're covering something up and have already lied about something, you might feel the need to continue lying. Escalation often accompanies a**holish behavior.

Some people are assholes just because. Sometimes we can't analyze them because we won't find out why. They might want control. They might have frustrations or enormous difficulties at home. They might be having a bad day. Maybe they stubbed their toe. If they're family members, bosses, or customers, we might be stuck interacting with them.

Habits, Triggers, and Pay-offs

Motives drive behavior. Habits drive behavior. Triggers affect behavior. Past trauma and pain influence behavior. Some people are highly sensitive or reactionary. Portraying a certain image impacts.

There are several reasons why a person is an asshole or occasionally acts like one. It could be that the person learned a way of being and has adopted a horrible way of relating to others. Others get some type of payoff from being a jerk. They feel satisfied about the attention or power. But they are never truly happy and keep playing the same game. After a while, they won't have too many friends, except other assholes.

Strengths and Weaknesses

Strengths and weaknesses can account for unkind behaviors. Some people brag about their talents and skills. They may tease others to show their superiority. Most of the time, "superiority" is a mask for feeling inferior. They may know they have a superior skill, but emotionally they feel inferior.

Some people are ashamed of their weaknesses to

the point where they don't want them exposed and don't want to feel vulnerable. We naturally don't like to showcase things we're not good at, so, for example, we hope we're not pressured into singing karaoke when we know we can't sing well. Some people go to the extreme to avoid exposing their weaknesses.

When someone develops anxiety and shame about their inadequacies or weaknesses, and if they fixate on them, they may be unkind to others so that they can feel superior. For example, a teenage boy with crooked teeth might make fun of other kids with an imperfect dental structure to elevate himself.

Personality Traits and Tendencies

Personality traits and the environment someone grows up in are very important in development. As we age, we come to know ourselves and we adopt coping mechanisms for the difficulties in life.

Our emotions and temperament play a role in what work we do, what activities we explore, and the type of people with whom we're comfortable. Personality inventories are great tools that reveal aspects of yourself that can aid you in social interactions.

In young adulthood, it's interesting to take personality tests and inventories. Sometimes we verify what we already know, and sometimes we make discoveries. Over the years, I've taken various personality inventories.

I've taken the long version (over 200 questions) of the Myers-Briggs Type Indicator (MBTI) five times since 1988 and consistently scored as an ENTJ type. I believe in the accuracy of the MBTI long version. ENTJs are at risk for neglecting people's feelings. The leadership style of an ENTJ includes an inflated sense of self and domineering tendencies. I recognize these areas as challenges.

Strengths Finder 2.0 by Tom Rath and *Emotional Intelligence 2.0* by Travis Bradberry and Jean Greaves are other helpful assessment tools. My results of the *Strengths Finder 2.0* assessment revealed that my strengths-based leadership style is strong in the areas of input, learner, ideation, strategic, and woo (winning others over). Each category discusses strengths from the standpoint of what profession or social scenario is optimal.

Examples are given, along with ideas for action, and what type of people the responder might be compatible with. I noticed a problem area with my "woo" strength. Winning others over is an extrovert characteristic that includes a cautionary observation. "You enjoy initiating with strangers because you derive satisfaction from breaking the ice and making a connection. Once that connection is made, you are happy to wrap it up and move on. There are new people to meet, new rooms to work, new crowds to mingle in. In your world, there are no strangers, only friends you haven't met yet – lots of them."

What sometimes happens is that I can appear superficial or not fully engaged in listening for a long period of time. I don't do this often and I try to avoid putting myself in situations where this could occur. *Strengths Finder 2.0* revealed a few things that were previously unknown to me as did *Emotional Intelligence 2.0*

Emotional Intelligence 2.0 provides an assessment for readers to understand and manage their emotions. This is vital in understanding behavior. Brain science indicates that one's first reaction is often an emotional one. We need to identify and control our emotions if we want to act civilly.

Emotional Intelligence 2.0 describes strategies for improvement in four areas: self-awareness, self-management, social awareness, and relationship management. I scored lower in the self-awareness category, and I saw clearly why I miss social cues and feel surprised about certain interactions and outcomes.

Looking at various assessments provides information about yourself that can be used as a tool for personal improvement and development. Although these inventories might not explain why someone is an a**hole, they aid in identifying traits and mannerisms.

3 HOW TO AVOID BEING AN A**HOLE

To avoid being an asshole, you need to determine if you're an asshole in the first place. Being on the receiving end of manipulation, gaslighting, abusive treatment, and other devious behaviors can trick someone into believing they're the perpetrators.

Most of the time, someone won't tell you if you're being an asshole. Consider it a gift if someone confronts you. You might not be aware that your words or actions are unwelcome. Pat yourself on the back if you figure out you've been mistreating someone and want to mend your ways.

I believe it's worse if you mistreat someone as opposed to someone mistreating you. When you mistreat someone, you've made an unkind decision or involuntary action. You may have contributed to bullying, belittling, criticizing, dismissing, abusing or devaluing someone.

If you're genuinely interested in making amends, you can apologize and contemplate how to change your offensive ways.

Consider the following clues: Do people stay away from you or avoid you? Do you cycle through several short-lived friendships or relationships? Do you have few friends even though you've tried to make friends? Do you get passed over for raises and promotions? Do you feel that those in higher positions seldom interact with you, and instead gravitate towards more likeable people?

Some of those questions don't indicate whether you're unkind or unlikeable, but could mean that you're shy or unassertive. People avoid people for various reasons.

Read through the following list and see if you have asshole tendencies.

You Might Be an Asshole If...

- One or more persons told you.

- Most people in a group setting avoid you.

- People are afraid of you.

- People scatter when you approach.

- You cycle through friends every few months or years.

- You can't name anyone you've been friends with for more than ten years.

- You can name several people who never want to see you again, after an unpleasant break up. Break up is not limited to romantic relationships. It can be family members, friends, or coworkers.

- You're aware that you've mistreated someone or caused that person harm.

- You have a pattern of saying unkind words and doing unkind things to people.

- You feel the need to be right and bulldoze over people.

- You want your way most of the time.

- You don't care about other people's feelings.

- You think you're smarter or better than others.

- You have more education, training or skills than those you interact with AND you have an elitist attitude about it. Actions follow attitudes.

- You meddle. You think you can help people who don't want your help or haven't asked for it.

- You micromanage. You don't allow others to shine or show their worth.

- You dominate over others. You're controlling, bossy, or aggressive.

- You interrupt or finish other people's sentences.

- You bait others by saying or doing things that embarrass or upset them.

- You're not helpful and you don't volunteer to help when help is desperately needed (and other acts of selfishness).

- You frequently refuse to compromise and make sacrifices.

- You brag, boast and enjoy talking about yourself.

- You think you're better than others and have little patience for listening to what you think is a waste of time.

- You're insecure and compensate by trying to bring others down.

- You're not very open-minded. You're eager to voice your opinions, and you don't fully listen to others.

- Someone calls you to discuss an issue or problem and you launch into something about yourself and then hang up when you're finished talking.

- Others know more about you than you know about them.

Being an A**hole is subjective. Ultimately, consider the interpersonal exchange and determine if you've been treated fairly and truthfully. Apologize if you're at fault.

The rest of the chapter describes how you can avoid being an a**hole.

Jealousy and Envy

Jealousy and envy are often confused and far be it for me to try to sort it all out. It's basically wanting what someone else has and experiencing a lack due to comparing.

I do know that I suffer from both envy and jealousy. Many times, I've longed for what others have, especially when it comes to skills and talents. I've wanted an easier life and things to go well, and used to look around and wonder why things didn't go as well for me as others.

As I age, I don't care. I count my blessings and realize that my life is different from everyone else's. I'm aware of my limitations. It's foolish for me to compare or complain. Instead, I just keep trudging along with the life I have, and guess what? Things aren't that bad. In fact, most of the time, things are great. I try to maintain a sense of humor I'm grateful for everything.

Common usage of both envy and jealousy has become such that both words are interchangeable. One definition of jealousy is as follows: resentment against a rival, a person enjoying success or advantage; mental uneasiness from suspicion or fear of rivalry, unfaithfulness; vigilance in maintaining or guarding something.

Envy is a feeling of discontent or covetousness regarding another's advantages, success, or possessions. Feelings of inferiority are strong with envy. For me, envy involves resentment and contempt for someone else's accomplishments or possessions to the point where I wouldn't mind the person failing in some way.

When I feel jealous, I experience insecurity, inadequacy, sometimes sadness, and sometimes anger. I do a lot of wishing and fantasizing. Jealousy often gets the best of me. I wish I were more like others in certain areas of my life. I don't wish them harm, but I often wonder how and why they have what I don't seem to have, and how can I be more like them?

Let's say you're overweight and haven't been able to shed a few pounds. Your friend lost 40 lbs. and you might outwardly wish her well, but secretly hope she gains the weight back because you haven't been able to lose the weight in over ten years. She looks great slim, but you're comfortable with her old self, with added weight. Maybe it's because you're disappointed in yourself that you haven't had success in weight loss and fear you can't lose weight. Your jealousy or envy stems from your insecurity and is unfair to her.

One reason I dropped out of social media was because I was comparing myself with others and watching their lives, or what they presented of their lives. I'm much better off not knowing what goes on in some people's lives because I want to avoid the trap of comparing. It's too painful and destructive.

Here's where jealousy and envy can lead to being an a**hole. You might gossip and talk about the person you're jealous of to someone else. You might end up with funky dynamics with someone you are jealous of. You might end up being inauthentic or not liking someone you previous liked simply because they are excelling or succeeding at something and in your mind, you're not.

Be a Good Person

The most important thing you can do is to be a person who doesn't provoke others, and who is likeable and kind. Don't be a burden on others. Make worthwhile contributions to the world. Don't cut the line; let others go before you.

Give more than you take. Keep your word. Be dependable and helpful. Don't make assumptions. Have reasonable expectations.

Keep working on emotional maturity. Is the person you present to the world and on social media quite different from the "real" you? Do you present an image or façade? If so, why? Explore why there is a big discrepancy in what you feel about yourself and what you reveal to others.

Inauthenticity involves concealment, distortion and deception.Being closed is different than being private. Purposely closing yourself off from others may involve arrogance, narcissism, and unkindness.

Mind Your Own Business

I've been known to meddle and ask too many personal questions when the recipient isn't interested in sharing. That's the price I pay for being an open person. I mistakenly think other people are open and comfortable discussing a myriad of topics.

You need to be aware of other people's sensitivities, privacy, and boundaries. And if someone encroaches on you, don't be timid to express your boundaries.

Be Quiet

Be quiet if you don't have anything to add to the conversation. Be quiet especially if your emotions are running away from you. Be quiet if someone is trying to provoke you.

Assert and defend yourself when warranted, but don't get entangled in a mess someone else is trying to start. And don't be the person who delights in provoking others.

Follow the non-violent communication technique and THINK before you speak.

You may say the wrong thing from time to time, but don't let your words, inappropriate comments, pride or ignorance stop you from creating optimal relationships.

Virtues and Morality

Morality refers to right and wrong. Can you imagine what kind of world we would have if everyone did the right thing? The court system would be nowhere near as busy as it is. We could eliminate half the lawyers. The same is true for social workers and police departments. Scammers and hackers would be non-existent. And wouldn't it be pleasant talking with people, knowing that there wasn't as much lying going on? Trust and respect would be on the rise.

Many of the world's social ills would be eliminated if people led a virtuous life. There are at least twenty virtues I can think of, but I'd like to describe ten.

- Integrity – adhering to sound moral and ethical principles

- Humility – a modest view of one's importance

- Charity – giving something to others in need; unselfish love and generosity

- Prudence – the habit of deciding well at each moment what one has to do; self-governance

- Chastity – the practice of using reason and restraint of the sexual instinct

- Temperance – moderation in action, thought or feeling

- Fortitude – strength of mind that enables a person to meet danger or bear pain or adversity with courage

- Diligence – careful or persistent work or effort

- Detachment – living simply and peacefully, avoiding whims and excess, while having a balanced temperament

- Obedience – following directives by adhering to what is right, good, or true

Check Your Ego at the Door

I get it. Some professions invite a big ego. But for most of us, in daily life, the overinflated ego is an unwelcome thing. Why are you so special? Why are you chosen? Why are you singled out? It must be nice to know it all. Excuse me. I'll take my little self and go off in the corner. I'm not important enough to be in your presence. Not that you notice anyway.

The world will tell you to pursue "the best version of yourself." This is rooted not only in goal accomplishment and success, but in ego and individualism. Of course, we should all be on a journey of improvement every day, without having to speak about it or draw attention to it. It seems like it's a given part of human existence. We don't want to go backwards, decline, or remain neutral. The obvious conclusion is to keep moving forward in all aspects of life.

I hope while people are seeking the best version of themselves, it means they are thinking of others along the way. As we climb higher and higher, to the top of a mountain, are we stepping on others along the way?

An overinflated sense of ego blocks the possibility to transcend the self and connect with others. There is a separation when there is ego. Those with big egos are not seeking unity, empathy or compassion.

Shift your energy away from the ego and embrace the concept of loving others. We can all win. We don't have to compete, dominate, or control.

Dr. Wayne Dyer once said EGO stands for Edging God Out. Don't be guilty of the pursuit of self at the expense of other important matters and people. What good is it if you're only serving yourself?

Another way to check to see If your ego has run amok is to ask, "What does the world need?" Many people focus on "What do I need and want?" The ego is set aside when we fill a need that provides value and meaning so that people can improve or transform their lives (unless the only reason for doing it is to get public accolades).

Kindness

The antidote to ego is kindness. Kindness anticipates the needs and desires of others and makes life more endurable. Kind actions are a way of doing "the right thing." Kindness offers hope and gratitude in the recipient. Where there is kindness, love expands within the giver and receiver. Love begets love. Kindness is contagious.

Think of the concept "pay it forward." Many people complain about the darkness in the world. Be a light and contribute to the contagiousness of kindness.

A healthy love of self precipitates kindness. If you don't like yourself, you might not be focused on charitable behavior. Kindness makes others feel good, special, encouraged or inspired. Kindness is a builder, whereas a**holeness is a destroyer.

The key to happiness is being kind to others, not striving for self-fulfillment while ignoring others.

Here are some examples of kindness:

* lend a listening ear

- drop what you're doing and focus on someone else

- do something you don't have to do

- fulfill your obligations

- be on time

- keep your word

- hold your tongue

- listen first and talk last

A person who lives an honorable life gravitates toward actions which build up humankind.

Embrace Your Ordinary Life

People who aren't comfortable with themselves or don't like themselves usually find a way to compensate. They may hide, drop out, stay within a small comfort zone, or present an image, which involves embellishment, deception and lying. Some unhappy souls take their anger, disappointment, and frustration out on others.

Being grateful, accepting yourself and your limitations, and liking yourself are insurance against being an a**hole. When we don't have anything to prove to anyone, we're content.

If you seek to do meaningful work, you won't feel average or inadequate. If you help others or serve others during your life, you can rest knowing you made a difference.

"Are You the Type…"

Take an inventory of your temperament, preferences, and personality traits.

Are you the type:

- To get angry easily? If yes, you're aggravating those around you. People will shut down and avoid you.

- To get triggered and spew? If yes, you need to work on managing your emotions.

- To talk too much? If yes, you're at risk for dominating conversations. You may be guilty of "speaking for others," interrupting, boasting, and poor listening habits. Talk less.

Do you want to avoid being an a**hole? Self-awareness, self-control, and social awareness are vital. Practice being a good, wholesome person.

PART II – PERCEPTIONS AND WORDS

4 MEAN GIRLS: THE PERPETRATOR AND THE VICTIM

Most of the time, we experience either being the a**hole (perpetrator) or being the recipient (victim). What happens when both roles play out at the same time? I'll give you an example of a painful experience I had in high school where the two intertwined.

Mean Girls

High school is a funky time. Students are no longer children, but not quite adults. It's a time of exploration and expansion. Teens are finding their way in a complicated, intimidating world, with many expectations thrust upon them. They are navigating who they are, what they want, and what they should do in the near and far future. They're experimenting with breaking rules, forging their identity, and contemplating possibilities.

Many haven't made the daunting decision or commitment about their future, yet they feel obligated to appease those well-meaning relatives and adults eager to inquire about the future of a person who is barely an adult. The common questions still are: "What's your SAT score? What college are you going to attend? What are you going to do when you graduate?"

Spring was in the air in early June, and I was a high school senior. One evening, a group of friends and I were going to go to a high school dance. The dances weren't the focus of the evening out, but a convenient opportunity to drink alcohol. In the early 1980's, the legal drinking age was 18 which means 16- and 17-year-olds found ways to purchase and consume alcohol. It was beneficial if someone in the group was 18 or older.

My friend Amanda had a boyfriend who was 18 and was kind enough to supply us with an assortment of alcohol. There might have been six or more of us partying that night. I invited my cousin Janey to join us. She was 17, like me, but was five feet tall and weighed about 95 pounds. She wasn't much of a drinker, but I could handle a decent amount of alcohol even though I was 107 pounds and 5'4." Little did I know that with a small amount of alcohol in her system, she would get very drunk in a short amount of time.

I picked up my stash of alcohol from Amanda's house and headed back home as I waited for my uncle to drop off Janey, who lived in another town.

The plan was for Janey and me to walk to Amanda's house and join the rest of the group later. We would do our drinking on our 30-minute walk, hang out at Amanda's for a while and walk the short distance to the school dance. Since this was a few decades ago, some details escape me, but I think our alcohol of choice was a bottle or two of apricot and blackberry flavored brandy.

It was a nice spring evening, and we set out on our stroll. We immediately began drinking and it wasn't long before our conversation became silly. Twenty or thirty minutes went by, and Janey was starting to slur and walk unevenly. I couldn't believe how quickly the alcohol was affecting her. Another few minutes and we had to cross a busy street. I deemed it too unsafe and told Janey I think we had better turn around and head back to my house.

At one point, Janey needed to lean on me for assistance as she stumbled along. Her speech became very slurred, and she was obviously staggering. Eventually she was deadweight, and I was annoyed at the situation in which I found myself. I was strong and able to escort her, albeit very slowly. I was disappointed at the turn of events because I imagined a fun night of partying. However, safety is most important even when you're sneaking around breaking rules.

At one point I noticed she was wearing only one clog. "Where's your other shoe?" I asked Janey. She was clueless that she had a missing shoe. We turned around and began looking for it in the dark. We were walking on a paved path through an apartment complex and in the dimly lit area, I saw no trace of the clog.

Oh well. We soon turned around and continued walking home. "Come on Janey, keep walking. We're almost there." It seemed to take hours to get back to my house, and during the time it took to arrive, I was concocting various stories to tell my mother.

Here we go, I thought. We walked through the door and my mother noticed Janey was heavily intoxicated. I think she was worried about the state Janey was in. Janey practically passed out and could barely speak. Alcohol poisoning is real. I knew she wasn't dangerously drunk, but my mother and uncle didn't like what they saw.

I didn't realize that Janey's father was going to wait for us. I was buzzed but composed. When they saw that Janey was ok, they hammered me with questions. I couldn't keep up with the frenzy, but I knew one thing: under no circumstances would I compromise my friends or provide the name of the 18-year-old who purchased the alcohol. He had nothing to do with the choices Janey and I made.

First and foremost, I didn't want to be a tattletale. I wasn't one to tattle on anyone. I endured enough hardship with a younger sister who frequently got me in trouble. I was a good liar and covered for others. I would hold my ground.

I was trying to stave them off from any details. I lasted at least 45 minutes, trying to provide enough information to get my mother and uncle off my back. Just take Janey home and go away, I thought. My mind was racing as to how I could tell half-truths and give them enough information so they would stop harassing me. My mother kept asking who bought the alcohol. She wanted a name, and she was relentless. She finally pulled it out of me, and I had to tell her it was James, Amanda's boyfriend.

If you remember high school, can you guess who is more important: the boyfriend/girlfriend, or the close friend? It's almost always going to be the teenage girl's boyfriend that takes priority over the good friend of three years.

My mother got on the phone that night and called Amanda's house, talking with her mother and trying to track down James. I pleaded with my mother not to get involved and stop calling my friend, and that nothing can be done. "I won't do it again. Please don't get my friend in trouble." Somehow the terrible night ended, and Janey went home, and I went to sleep. But the problems for me were just beginning. My life was about to turn upside down.

At school on Monday, Amanda asked "How could you do that? James could get in trouble." "I had no choice. My mother forced it out of me," I pleaded. Amanda scoffed, "You didn't have to tell." "I'm sorry. I had no choice. I stalled for 45 minutes, but I kept getting pestered by my mother and uncle."

The conversation wasn't going anywhere. I felt terrible. I had betrayed my friends. Amanda didn't want to hear my explanation or excuses. I violated the rules of friendship by snitching and potentially causing an arrest. She turned and stomped away.

Later that day as I was changing into my softball uniform, Amanda's friend Jessie, snickered at me and asked why I was wearing an elf uniform. "You look like an elf." I told her it was a sports uniform. "Look at those shoes!" she laughed as she pointed at my cleats. She was a very feminine person, who paid attention to trends, wearing the latest fashion, and an inch of makeup on her face. I don't think she knew what sports were, let alone the fact that uniforms went along with team sports.

The next day I felt cold stares from two more of Amanda's friends, Darcy and Caroline. I was beginning to feel like an outcast for being forced by my mother to tell her James bought the alcohol. Later in the day while at my locker, Darcy came up to me and smiled, "I hear you're pregnant. There are rumors going around." "Who told you?" I wanted to know. Of course, she didn't answer but just smirked at me and strutted away, with her head held high.

I kept a straight face. I was a virgin and wasn't involved with any guys, so of course there was zero truth in that. I thought to myself though, how does one deny and protect oneself from a rumor like that? Once again, I felt defeated and helpless.

I was beginning to not like Amanda and the rest of my so-called friends. How could they turn on me in a split second? Never ever mess with a teenage girl's boyfriend. It's as if I ruined Amanda's life. I'm sure she thought I was an asshole, and she wasn't going to let it go.

Let's pause for a moment in this story and point out that from Amanda's perspective, I was an a**hole for telling on her boyfriend. She probably got in trouble and maybe it caused a conflict between her and James. He could get arrested, so there was a lot at stake. Amanda probably reasoned that I was a horrible person and thought I should have kept quiet.

Her life and relationship could be ruined, and how could I do that? She was probably so angry that she wanted to get back at me or make my life miserable, since I made her life miserable.

The last two weeks of the school year were pure hell. Amanda was through with me, I could tell, and the group of friends didn't associate with me anymore. Fortunately, I had a few good friends that weren't part of Amanda's Mean Girls Clique. I wasn't completely lonely, but the sting was raw and real and there was no way for me to repair the situation.

I thought I was a nice person, and at that point in my life, I was not familiar with causing problems or being severed from a friendship. It was foreign to me, and I didn't know what to do with those emotions. When your friend doesn't want to listen, you have no choice but to pick yourself up and begin anew. Proceed in a new direction.

Final exams were administered at the same time we were supposed to return our books for the year. I thought I left a few textbooks in my locker, but they weren't there. Hmm, where did I put them? Did I leave them at home? I checked at home and couldn't locate them. I told the teachers I had no idea where they were and that I was certain they were in my locker. Something was unusual. If I couldn't find them within the next few days, I would need to pay a small fee for each book.

Graduation came and went, and it was a wonderful celebration and party afterwards. I was excited to start college in an exciting city in a few months.

During my freshman year of college, I kept my part time high school job at a convalescent home in town and worked a few shifts during breaks and holidays. I was happy to see Brenda during the fall, a high school friend who also worked at the convalescent home. She was a year younger than me and in her senior year. She and I were friends even though she was a part of the Mean Girls Clique.

We were talking about how I liked college and what her plans were for the coming year. Brenda wanted to tell me something about Amanda.

Brenda told me how one night in June, soon after the dance debacle, Amanda and the group gathered around a fire and burned my books! Amanda had stolen them from my locker, which I left unlocked for ease of grabbing books in between classes.

I felt strange hearing this. I wasn't angry, but calm. I felt violated. That's how I feel when something is stolen from me. Violated. Someone is watching or plotting to steal your belongings. It's a creepy feeling.

But to make a bonfire! I thought that was weird. I thanked Brenda for sharing and told her I wasn't surprised they would do something like that.

I hadn't realized how much rage fueled the mean girls desire to perform some bizarre and hateful act. I really was an a**hole in their minds. Well, on the flip side, they were a**holes to me. While I was going through it, it was excruciating. As soon as I got out of the environment, the whole incident was a nonissue to me.

I forgot about them, forgave them and the mean girls didn't occupy any place in my mind. I had no animosity or bad feelings about those high school girls. They weren't part of my life, and I'd probably never see them again. I was too busy building my exciting new life in college in preparation for my career.

I had no contact or desire to interact with those former friends. Their values didn't align with mine. I moved away from home after graduating high school and loved my new life in a big city, at an amazing university. I was happy to be away from my hometown, which I summed up in four words: "small town, small minds."

I returned to my home of origin during college breaks. During adulthood, I visited once every year or so, and more often when I lived in New York. Later, there were times when I hadn't visited my hometown for five or seven years.

I remember seeing Amanda at high school reunions and I don't think either one of us had resentment. 17-year-olds in high school are immature and I'm sure we both matured well beyond what transpired years ago.

Decades went by and I moved to my current home in a new state, 30 minutes away from a good high school friend named Didi. Didi was good friends with Amanda, but not part of the mean girls' clique.

In 2015, Didi was invited to visit Amanda who was on vacation in our area. Didi asked me if I'd like to come for the evening and I said yes. Didi wasn't aware of the high school tiff I had with Amanda, and my feelings toward Amanda were neutral. I was comfortable.

Another mutual high school friend, Olga, planned on showing up. Olga is a dear friend of mine, and I'd kept in touch and visited Olga on several occasions since graduating high school. Didi and I had sporadic contact and have become closer since I moved within 30 minutes of where she lives.

Both Olga and Didi kept in touch with Amanda over the years. I wasn't interested in keeping in touch with Amanda after high school but heard about her from time to time. I was busy building my career in my twenties and my family in my thirties and forties. I kept in touch with Olga, Didi and one other high school friend. I hadn't given Amanda much thought.

Before the dance debacle, Amanda and I were close friends and shared many great adventures in our teen years. I was looking forward to seeing Amanda and catching up. It went well and was a fun evening. Between 2015 and 2022, I saw or spoke with Amanda a few times. I enjoyed reconnecting.

Soon after Amanda moved to the state in 2022, the four of us met for lunch. A new idea was percolating. Maybe we could get together for a weekend. It would take some planning since we live in different parts of the state. We've done this at least three times and are planning one this year.

Amanda is likeable, interesting, and fun, and when people know my story, they wonder why I'm friends with her.

I tell them this: the incident for me was forgotten and forgiven several months after it happened. I give no energy to it and harbor no ill feelings. I understand that when you're 17- years-old, you do ridiculous things. I certainly hope that if I've been a twit to someone that they realize with the passage of time people change. Some malicious chronic a**holes don't seem to change, but there's hope for occasional ones like me.

I recounted the details of this story to demonstrate that one's perspective impacts and determines if someone is an a**hole. Amanda and I haven't discussed the drinking and dance story. We don't need to. Our friendship is based on who we are today. I was attracted to her outgoing and fun personality in 10th grade, and she still enlivens me.

Amanda is a great storyteller, complete with unique hand gestures and colorful body language. She's multi-talented, with a lot of smarts, wisdom, and commonsense. If I harbored resentment for decades, I'd miss out on so much.

Bottom Line

- Perspective differs and matters.

- Sometimes we unintentionally appear as an a**hole to others. They in turn might respond by being an a**hole to us. Don't fall into this trap of retaliation or revenge.

- Being an a**hole brings out the worst in you and others.

- People are at risk for deviating from their foundational values and behaviors when pushed over the edge.

- Forgiveness is optimal and loving. Forgiveness restores balance and neutrality. Forgiveness sets you free and opens a pathway to positivity.

5 FOOT-IN-MOUTH DISEASE

There are two ways you can be an a**hole: by your words and/or by your actions. Let's take a close look at the importance of the words we say to others. Words come from our thoughts. Not only do our thoughts need to be monitored and sanitized, but our words do too.

Watch Your Words

Words matter. Words can be hurtful. Words can be uplifting. The popular phrase "THINK before you speak" can serve as a guide. THINK stands for the following words: True, Helpful, Inspiring, Necessary, and Kind. We should not speak unless it meets the following criteria: Is what you are about to say true, helpful, inspiring, necessary, and/or kind? Use this as a quick checklist before you open your mouth.

As I've gotten older, I've gotten less talkative and more observant. I don't automatically make verbal offerings unless I feel I can add to the conversation. I'm more apt to speak if I sense my words will be appreciated and helpful. I used to offer a lot of information and advice. I also wanted to be heard, after spending years as a quiet, shy child.

These days, I'm more selective. I share my insights with those who are interested and willing to make an investment of time by listening with a possible intent to incorporate my suggestions into their lives. I'd rather add insight or entertainment to others' lives rather than add clutter and mutter.

Slowing down and responding thoughtfully are important in communication. I'm still working on not reacting if I feel provoked. My goals are to interrupt less, listen more, and have patience during conversations. I'm guilty of being blunt and saying things that I shouldn't. That's the price I pay for being talkative and not editing my thoughts before they spill over during conversation. I admit to awkward and unkind situations.

I try to select kind words to say, and if I feel unkind, I aim to refrain from speaking. Editing yourself can stop you from saying something you might regret. Take a few breaths, delay a second or two with silence, and proceed slowly with your words if you're feeling unhealthy emotions forming.

Can you think of a time when you were hasty with your words? I'd like to share two incidents that happened in my early twenties and a few more from later years when I was unwise with my words.

Overweight Cadet

I was a Reserve Officers' Training Corps (ROTC) cadet, stationed for six weeks at Ft. Knox, KY, training to become a military officer. This was decades ago and I'm sorry I was critical of an overweight cadet. I was talking with someone else about the overweight person and how it's a matter of good habits and avoidance of a sloppy, overeating lifestyle that causes it and that he should do something about it.

I received a long, handwritten note from the overweight cadet saying how insensitive I was and that he has struggles that he's addressing. I felt compassion for the guy and disappointment in myself for being so harsh.

Bottom Line

- THINK before you speak. I made unnecessary and unkind comments.

- Arrogance. I demonstrated a superior and know-it-all attitude, the makings of an a**hole.

- None of my business. What I hoped to accomplish (a change in behavior from someone else) is not my place, especially since I didn't know the person and probably wouldn't see him again.

Drunk Driver Privileges

I served as an S-1/ Personnel Officer for a military unit and was privy to various professional and personal happenings of the people in the battalion. One Lieutenant told me he was arrested for a DUI (Driving Under the Influence) and said he got a good lawyer that dismissed the charges for a hefty fee.

I said, "Wow, so if you have money, you can have the case dropped and avoid responsibility? I don't like that. What if you caused an accident or death?" He was quiet and I realized that I didn't need to say that.

Bottom Line

- Keep your thoughts to yourself if they aren't helpful and if they are scathing.

- What I said was rude and uncalled for.

- It was none of my business to judge him for getting a good lawyer for his defense.

- Even if someone does something dishonest or unlawful, who appointed me an enforcer?

They Don't Like You

Foot-in-Mouth Disease doesn't affect us only when we're younger. It can haunt us throughout our lifetime if we don't take measures to clean up our language. I've been guilty of rude words in recent years.

While visiting two high school friends at the beach, Amanda and Didi, I told them of my recent trip to our hometown where 13 alumni got together. Didi asked, "Why did they have a get together for you?"

I told her that when an alum plans on visiting our hometown from out of state, the visitor can reach out via social media and announce they're coming. A local friend coordinates a date and time for the gathering at a popular restaurant and sends out an informal invitation to former classmates.

I decided to contact a graduate who lives in our hometown and ask if we can get together. When Didi asked why they arranged a meeting for me, I replied, "Maybe they don't like you."

What an unkind thing to say to someone! Didi was quiet the rest of the evening and when I spoke with her a few days later, she told me how she felt and said she didn't appreciate me saying that. I apologized and felt terrible for making assumptions.

Didi and I have been friends for many years. I thanked her for pointing out something I was clueless about. Now I have a new awareness, and better manners.

Bottom Line

- Arrogance. I was unintentionally comparing myself to Didi and thought I was more likeable by certain classmates. That isn't true at all.

- Edit your thoughts before they become spoken words. Many times, thoughts will pop into our head. Don't verbalize thoughts that don't follow the THINK model.

- We need to work on changing our insensitive

thoughts to kind thoughts, or we risk making insensitive comments. We need to think about unity and connection with others.

No Tip for You, Pizza Man

I needed the help of my father-in-law to manage the arrival of my husband at a certain time for his 40th surprise birthday party. The plan was for them to go out on his birthday, which was on a Thursday night, and return home at a carefully selected time.

Guests were asked to arrive between 6:15 and 6:30 pm. I ordered four large pizzas to be delivered at 7:00 pm. They repeated the order to me; I hung up the phone and was happy that everything was going well.

My husband was supposed to arrive at 7:00 pm and when the time passed by, there was no pizza and no husband. I called the pizza place around 7:15 and they said they had no record of an order for me, so I sighed and ordered four more. Another 45-minute wait.

Meanwhile, I could sense that some of the guests wanted to leave because it was a weeknight, and they probably thought two hours was an adequate investment in time for the party.

My husband and father-in-law arrived at 8:00 pm and I asked my father-in-law why they were so late. He said they were having a good time, and he didn't want to cut their time short. The pizzas arrived soon after.

When the pizza delivery man showed up, I walked outside and expressed my disappointment by saying something like, "I won't be leaving a tip because I've been trying to get the pizzas for an hour and a half. Timing was important for this party."

He had nothing to do with the timing. He looked at me dumbfounded. He's a delivery guy whose job to deliver the pizzas was separate from the store operations. He probably didn't know my order was forgotten and had no idea why I was angry.

I would never treat someone so poorly today.

Bottom Line

- Unrealistic expectations. I expected excellent service from the restaurant. They made a mistake, and I was intolerant of the mistake.

- I blamed an innocent person and mistreated him. The delivery guy was an employee who was following orders. He had nothing to do with the customer order process.

- I could have turned the mishap into an opportunity. I could have tipped him well and thanked him, assuming that the restaurant was busy, or short-staffed, trying to complete an overabundance of orders that night. The pizzas arrived hot, fresh, and were very good quality.

- That night an employee encountered an ungrateful, complaining, angry woman.

Good Thing You Chose Me

Many years ago, I was part of the homeschool community. Sam and Sarah, the leaders of our local homeschool support group, were taking an extended vacation, and they wanted to find a substitute leader. At the end of a meeting, I was talking with the couple about it in private, or so I thought.

I said, "Yeah, I think I should fill in while you're gone because we share the same values and I don't think Dan and Jan would be a good choice." Within seconds of saying that, Dan rounded the corner, and I was stunned, not sure if he heard what I said.

I was good friends with Dan and Jan, but I felt the need to voice my superiority for the job to serve as temporary leader of the group. The next day, Jan called me and said she didn't like the comment I made, and I explained why I said it and apologized. It didn't matter. Sometimes your words leave an indelible mark, and the damage is beyond repair. That was the last time I heard from Jan and Dan.

There goes another friendship.

Bottom Line

- Superiority. Definitely an a**holish quality.

- I should have learned the lesson before age 35 that I will lose good friends if I talk about them negatively and especially if they heard what I said. That is also true if someone told them what I said.

- I insulted them and they saw my true colors when I made religion an issue when it had nothing to do with anything and it was a judgmental comment.

- Over the years, I've had to work on my attitude and comments. Words matter and if you want friends, you need to be kind to them and think highly of them. You need to respect them and treat them well. THINK before you speak and avoid Foot-in-Mouth Disease.

6 HOLD YOUR TONGUE

I can think of many other situations where I thought being honest was better than keeping quiet. Sometimes that gets me in trouble! Is it our duty to keep peace over everything else? Are we obligated to draw attention to important (important to who?) matters? These are things we must sort out.

We must also continue to work on improving our communication skills. Many people will report a breakdown in marriage and relationships due to "irreconcilable differences" or a failure to communicate. The non-violent communication style is something that might save your marriage and relationships.

The final secret to holding your tongue is to adopt a calm demeanor and spirit of meekness. Silence is a virtue and listening to understand will bring peace to any interaction.

Just Because it's True Doesn't Mean You Should Say It

A friend and her newly married, pregnant daughter were visiting. We were talking about people who change their names, and the daughter said she identifies as non-binary and goes by another name. I wanted to say, "Well, you're married to a man now and expecting a baby, so I hope you consider yourself heterosexual." I couldn't say what I was thinking because at that moment my husband entered the room, wasn't aware of the conversation in progress, and I thought it would be inappropriate to voice my opinion.

As the minutes went by, I decided that it was good that I didn't say anything. I thought about the purpose of sharing my thoughts and opinions and it's to influence change in others. But maybe the point of our conversations isn't to insert anything, or to influence change, but to simply go with the flow of congenial relations. Listen to what matters to the other person.

Aside from this incident, I'm trying to choose silence more often than "righteousness." In my twenties and thirties, I thought speaking up was helpful and the preferred path. Now that I'm older, I find that it's not worth it most of the time. It depends. If you have a vested interest or investment in a relationship, AND if people are receptive, then I would suggest putting forth more effort, but for acquaintances and people you don't see too often, let it go. Who cares? So what?

Being Pushy

Making our opinions known or trying to get our way can involve trampling over others. We might not be open-minded or effective listeners when we have a goal in mind. We can be insensitive and unreasonable in the other person's view. I think I'm guilty of this with Maggie.

In a more recent encounter, my daughter needed a new car. I called a dealership and spoke to a salesperson, in detail, about what she wanted. He said her car could probably qualify for a $7,000 trade-in, and that it would be in demand for college students in the area. He asked us to meet him at the dealership that day. I told him we were coming in for a specific model and wanted to look at a few cars that appeared on the dealership's website.

The process was long and drawn out. First, he didn't know where the used models we wanted to see were located. Next, the website was outdated and the three models we wanted to see weren't there. He offered no explanation about it. I made comments like, "The dealership should keep the website information current unless the cars sold within a few hours."

He showed us cars with body damage and said that repairs would be made after a purchase. He showed us a dirty car that was dropped off at the dealership and wasn't processed through, with no price or information sticker. He asked us what we wanted to pay for it! Strange. His goal was to sell us a car. He wasn't listening to our requests.

When we were test driving a car, I suspect I made obnoxious comments because he suddenly got quiet. I said we wouldn't be buying a car today because we didn't want a damaged car, and he also couldn't answer specific questions I had about the cars. He had no notebook with information on the VIN numbers and couldn't tell us about the history of the vehicle.

When we got back to his desk, he showed us the numbers and costs of various cars. Earlier on the phone, I told him our price range, and at our meeting, he didn't consider that at all. He was persuading us to purchase something beyond our budget. Plus, he said there was a $4,000 required dealer's warranty. We said we didn't want it. He told us we had no choice. I said, "If I had known this, we would not have wasted your time or ours. I'm not paying an additional $4,000 for a used car."

The offer for our trade-in? $1,500. Next, he pitched us the idea of leasing a vehicle. He told us about an exciting program at the dealership. The sales associates had goals to sell a certain number of cars so that they would win an award. What were the perks for the customers? Where was the consideration for what the customer wanted? A salesperson can make a sale if he is able to present the prospective buyer with a close match to what the customer is looking for. None of that happened.

He acted like we hurt his feelings. He wasn't fully honest. I told him about my requirements on the phone earlier in the day before even arriving at the dealership. If he had intentions of following through with what he discussed with me on the phone, the interaction would have been completely different.

His words were empty and meaningless. The offer for my daughter's vehicle was a lot lower than he led me to believe. He didn't have any decent used cars to show us. He disregarded our price range. He didn't answer why the vehicles on the website weren't available for sale. He had no notebook, roster, or information to provide.

I was brutally honest, and I thought clear communication would be appreciated, but it was ignored. We were ignored. I didn't want to play along with the game. I felt insulted by the salesman on a few occasions. I suppose he didn't like me, and I didn't care for his unprofessional manner.

My daughter and I have PTSD from this experience, and I don't know if I ever want to purchase another car from a dealership again. He was pushy. I was pushy. We were communicating in opposite directions. We were both a**holes. I could have acted nicer, even if he was misbehaving. I could have chosen to be quiet and excuse myself sooner.

I don't think I was provoked. The salesperson didn't bring out the best in me, and we were adversaries. A salesperson who strikes up an adversarial relationship probably won't be making a sale with a prospective customer.

Last year, two of my young adults purchased their cars through Carvana, which carries a seal of approval for the mechanical condition of the car. The price you pay is the sticker price, plus taxes. It's been a year, and their cars are in great shape and operating well. I have high trust in Carvana.

They let you know if there's an additional fee, such as a shipping fee from another location. There are no hidden or added costs, and the process is respectful and smooth, for the most part.

We had another highly favorable transaction with another car company. My son purchased a new electric car with a reputable company and the process was extremely professional, transparent, efficient, and easy. No fuss, no muss, no a**holes.

Non-Violent Communication (NVC)

Developed by Dr. Marshall Rosenberg in the 1960's, non-violent communication (NVC) is a communication style which portrays compassion, kindness, and respectful treatment of others. Patient listening is a crucial component as well as expressing needs in a gentle manner.

Dr. Rosenberg traveled the world sharing his NVC techniques, which resulted in successful outcomes in various companies, communities, and nations. NVC was instrumental in desegregating schools in the Southern United States.

Dr. Rosenberg uses a model of the jackal and the giraffe in some of his instructional videos. The jackal represents communication that is aggressive, heated, and selfish. The giraffe is gentle and patient. Non-violent communication offers a win-win outcome, where both parties strive for understanding and compatible resolution.

The four-part process is worth examining in the official non-violent communication literature.

Basically, the listener presents his or her perspective and states an **observation** and **feelings** that pertain to the observation using "I" statements. The listener proceeds to state his or her **needs** and makes a **request**. The other person then responds.

Much of what passes for communication in our culture is sadly centered on jackal-type interactions and is partly habitual and partly learned. I encourage you to learn the four-step process of non-violent communication. This can change your marriage and your life. I learned about this technique more than 25 years ago and it's made a difference in my marriage and interactions. Basically, you state your observation, share how you feel, express your need, and make a request.

Here's a recent example. My husband and I were in a restaurant with my son and his girlfriend. The check arrived, and my husband was ready to pay. I saw the suggested tipping column was 5% above the customary average, and I'm tired of the increasing tipping culture. My husband is generous and frequently pays above the tip average, even with inadequate service.

I made a negative comment about the high tip suggestion, and he repeated what I said in a sarcastic voice. I experienced it as contempt. It was loud enough for others at our table (and beyond) to hear. I felt a sting and I felt embarrassed. I think my husband felt criticized, but that was not my intention.

I said something like, "I'm tired of our tipping culture." Next time, if I sense that he feels criticized,

I will ask him on the spot and clarify my comments. I didn't intend personal criticism, but rather a tipping culture criticism. If the average rate is 20%, I didn't like seeing 20, 22, and 24% suggestions. My comments were of a broad nature about our culture.

NVC is not just about meeting our needs but being in tune with what others think and feel as well.

Here's what I said: "I hear you using a sarcastic tone about the tip (observation). I was expressing my dissatisfaction, and I feel that your response was a mocking tone (feelings). I don't like it, and I feel it's a form of contempt. Can you please not do that (request)?" He immediately apologized and realized he had made an impulsive response (probably because he felt criticized).

I didn't expand on my need at the restaurant, but my husband knows I don't like to be spoken to in a mocking tone. I implied my need in what I said to him. I could have said more, but I wanted to keep my comments brief at the restaurant. Later, when we were home, I brought the topic up so we could discuss the matter in private, and he did feel criticized.

Can you see how long, drawn out, and tedious communicating this way might be, especially if your communication style is more abrupt? It does take a while to master, and it feels probing. It feels as if you're saying far too many words than necessary for a conversation.

What I've noticed is that if you work through this technique for several weeks and months, you'll begin to master the process without thinking about it and you'll end up using less words. It won't seem as arduous as it was in the beginning. As with any skill, it takes practice.

How has NVC improved our 40-year marriage? My husband and I can be headstrong at times, but we are quick to yield to each other and consider different viewpoints. We come to a consensus amicably, make enthusiastic compromises, and understand how to handle differences. It also helps that we understand the value of influencing each other and have a high level of respect for each other.

When we depart from relationship-health, it's usually for a moment and very short-lived. Neither of us wants a tense or unfulfilling marriage, so we're good at repairing and restoring our friendship when things go awry. Successful relationships are a result of continuous care.

We slip away from NVC when we let our strong emotions intensify at the beginning of the interaction. Tips: Talk with each other in the same room, make eye contact, slow down your thoughts and rate of speaking, take a deep breath, say a silent momentary prayer, and take turns speaking and listening.

Walk away if you're both not ready to discuss the issue calmly and lovingly. Return later when you're receptive. The four-step process might take a few weeks or months to feel comfortable because you're developing a new style and changing habits.

The ideal would be for more people to use non-violent communication in their exchanges. We would decrease our a**hole interactions if we adopted non-violent communication. Say goodbye to the jackal (or jackass) and hello to the giraffe.

Life Doesn't Work That Way

Some of us believe in karma, revenge or retaliation if we've been mistreated. I'm guilty of this. When someone says cruel things to me, my first thought is to defend myself in my mind and sometimes out loud. My second thought is to "get even" with the other person. My third thought is to ponder if there's any truth to the comment. I also consider the source and wonder the speaker's purpose for the comment.

My experience with retaliation is that it often backfires or doesn't reap satisfying results. One day, my daughter made a snarky comment, and I didn't like being disrespected, but I didn't confront her. Instead, I retaliated and said something impulsive and rude. My granddaughter kept asking for me, and my daughter wondered, "Why doesn't she want to come to me? I said, "Because I'm gentle and you're aggressive." Silence.

I knew before I said it, that it was unkind and unnecessary, even if it was true. I felt terrible saying it. My motivation was to get back at her or to feel a sense of power, which is immature and reactionary.

It doesn't matter if someone is being unkind to you. It doesn't justify unkindness in return, but this is what often happens. Mistreatment festers and grows, and we each have the power to stop it with humility and emotional strength.

Choosing meekness is not choosing weakness;

it's choosing peace and kindness. Holding your tongue is one of the smartest things you can do in life.

PART III – MOVING FORWARD

7 TAKE RESPONSIBILITY

When you let someone go or are considering it, do it with compassion and diplomacy. When someone lets you go, you must decide the best way to handle it.

After you've acted unkindly, take time to reflect on your shortcomings and make corrections in the future. Try to see things from another person's perspective. Take accountability for your objectionable words and actions.

"A gentleman is one who never inflicts pain." – John Henry Cardinal Newman

When we cause pain, we must take responsibility for our action. Taking responsibility means making attempts to repair something that's broken or not in balance. Think of it as a restoration project.

Maggie

Maggie let me go, I assumed, because she felt criticized. She expressed her dissatisfaction, and for her, it was probably "the last straw." Although I felt she let me go for one reason, there were other things she might not have liked about me. Another possibility she let me go is that I'm nosy and opinionated. I know I'm a little loose and free with my opinions. Perhaps I meddled in issues that were none of my business.

Although you may be deepening your friendship, you must proceed gently as you enter increasingly personal subjects. I'm an open person who sometimes doesn't gauge the sensitivity of others, especially when a person is highly private or closed.

I also might have fallen short of her expectations by not participating in some outings. I didn't go along with some of her adventures because I was fatigued. Maybe she believed I was unreliable, disagreeable, or selfish for not tagging along.

As the dumped friend, I'm going to conclude that my friend viewed me as out-of-line, insensitive, opinionated, opportunist, selfish, and at times, inauthentic – qualities that constitute an a**hole. It's hard to see myself that way because I believe I don't act in those ways, but if I ask, "Am I the A**hole?" then the answer is yes.

Sometimes we can build a case in our mind about the person who dumps us. I began to do that. I noticed that Maggie wasn't really interested in most things about me, or the important things about my life except for outdoor adventure activities we shared. She focused mainly on the few things we had in common.

When I brought up projects I was working on in other areas of my life, she showed no interest. On the other hand, I was impressed and fascinated with her life and the conversation would often center on that. Perhaps I found her more interesting than she found me.

As you've probably noticed, I've done a lot of guesswork about my friendship with Maggie. I spent time wondering why things ended the way they did, and why the friendship completely ended in the first place.

At some point though, when you've been let go, you must stop wondering and simply accept the situation.

I could have attempted to reach her again and asked why she didn't return my calls. However, I needed to be prepared for brutal honesty, and I didn't want to endure that.

"Come from a space of peace and you'll find that you can deal with anything." – Michael A. Singer

Marcus

During the first two years of our friendship, I enjoyed assisting Marcus with writing letters to community leaders, taking him on errands, and socializing with him. He had interesting perspectives and humorous quotes.

He was handicapped and couldn't drive, and I volunteered to take him places twice a week. I did this for three years and it was fine for a while. But there came a time when the season ended, and I let him go.

I didn't want to tell him what bothered me. There was no easy or kind way to say that I didn't want to interact with him.

I no longer wanted to spend time with him because his opinions and monologues about politics were boring and annoying. At first, I was polite and listened, but the topic dominated our conversations, and I had no interest in politics. I told him, but he persisted.

His persecution complex and paranoia wore me down and I couldn't say anything to change or calm that. Marcus depleted my energy. I would arrive at his house in good spirits with high energy and after we reached our destination in just fifteen minutes, I was fatigued!

Toward the end of my friendship with Marcus, he kept asking why I no longer wanted to drive him places and do things with him. I told him I just didn't want to, or that I was focusing on various goals and projects.

He passed away two years ago, and I occasionally think about him and miss him. He was a godly man, with a kind heart, and solid values. He suffered tremendous physical and emotional pain and is now free of that.

"A kind heart is a fountain of gladness, making everything in its vicinity freshen into smiles." – Washington Irving

Self-Improvement

Here are a few techniques you can try as you move toward healthy relations.

1. Don't justify that you no longer want this friend in your life. Instead, bring the focus back to what you said or did to create a change of attitude in your former friend. Focus on the incident(s), and the effect it had on you, the offended person, rather than find fault in the other person.

2. Sometimes it's not your fault. Own it if it's something small or easy to smooth over. It's better to keep the peace than to continue an argument that can last hours, days or years. If the person's perception is that you did something objectionable, then treat the encounter as if they're right. Note: This assumes that the person is reasonable and of sound mind, and not a scheming, manipulative, gaslighting narcissist.

3. If it's your fault, take responsibility, ask forgiveness, and especially clarification. Many difficulties are misunderstandings. You'll discover that you need to move in another direction and let a relationship go if it drains you or you feel you're making heroic efforts.

4. If you've been discarded or feel the need to move on, pick a fresh new card from the deck and work on yourself. Taking responsibility for your words and actions will help you repair problems in relationships and deter you from offending others in the first place.

"Kindness should be a frame of mind in which we are alert to every opportunity: to do, to give, to share and to cheer." – Patricia Bragg

8 FORGIVE AND MOVE ON

Let's talk about forgiveness. Forgiveness is helpful for both the perpetrator and the victim, when you've offended others and when you've been harmed.

Admit and Accept

I've talked about this before, but you cannot forgive unless you understand, admit, and accept what happened. There comes a time when we need to acknowledge that we acted in unacceptable ways and the person no longer cares to associate with us.

We're not as great as we think we are! Some people find us likeable, and others want little to do with us. When we've been dumped, we need to forgive ourselves. We need to forgive others, and we need to let go. Let it go into the air and let God do what He wills because we have no control over the outcome.

Let them be. Let them be free of us and we can invest our time in other endeavors and other people.

It's hard to admit that being fired from a job wasn't personal. Sometimes being released is a gift. It's an opportunity for reflection, growth, and a new direction.

We will enter various seasons of life. The changing seasons bring different people, places, adventures, jobs, hobbies, and activities. Nothing lasts forever and everything is temporary. When you've been dumped, or if you find yourself recovering from challenges, adopt some new hobbies.

Move your body and hands. Physical movement brings forth physical change and boosts brain health. Get involved in community service or volunteerism. Do things that help you feel worthy and productive. I've embraced two new artistic hobbies and it's bringing me great joy to give away some of my creations, especially when everyone is appreciative. My wares are becoming conversational pieces too!

When you can admit your wrongdoing and accept the consequences of your a**holeness, you free yourself and create space to treat others better.

Why it's Important to Forgive

Authentic forgiveness is an act of humility and charity. It's not easy to forgive because we must embrace vulnerability and let go of pride, self-righteousness, and self-protection. Forgiveness is complicated if we have expectations. Forgiveness is a gift that is given and received.

Oftentimes, there are different assumptions between the two parties. One may feel that a person doesn't deserve forgiveness. One may feel that the person isn't remorseful, or the situation may never change. Thus, some believe forgiveness must be earned and deserved.

One may ask for forgiveness and not receive it. Some prefer to offer a "conditional" type of forgiveness. The best thing you can do is to do "the right thing." Search your heart and conscience for the right thing. Hopefully compassion and reason will guide you.

When we forgive others, we let go of negative emotions. We lighten our burden, and we can lighten the burden of another. Forgiveness is an act of freedom. Forgiveness also leads to kindness, understanding, and compassion. It contributes to a peaceful world.

I have a secret to share. You might think that the a**hole has no conscience and doesn't care and is forgetful of his or her heinous acts. That's not true. Memories and consciences are present in everyone. Many people think that the victim, the one who has been harmed, remembers the mistreatment. Not necessarily. This is why acceptance of the act(s) and forgiving oneself and others lessens the preoccupation.

Reaching the point of forgiveness can be difficult in situations where tremendous harm has been done. I was greatly wronged more than 20 years ago, and I don't think I've fully forgiven the people involved who built an unfair case against me. I fully believe I was the victim of sexual harassment, and my career suffered due to poor employee performance appraisals written by my boss who targeted me.

As a result, I was not promoted or given increased responsibility. Within two years, I landed a new job, and my new senior managers were astonished that I was thwarted in my early career. I quickly advanced and was respected, unlike the horrendous circumstances I'd experienced a few years prior.

When I reminisce about my earlier job hardship, I haven't completely forgiven those involved in my downfall. For several years, I secretly hoped that those who harmed me experienced "karma." I don't expect to see them again, and over the years I've occasionally tried to locate some of the perpetrators. One senior employee met with an early death after a chronic health issue. I couldn't locate the main perpetrator, but I imagined that he had a lonely, unhappy life.

Can you see what unresolved contempt can do? It left a lingering residue. My imagination about those twits was negative. What good does that do?In a warped way, I felt somewhat powerful and triumphant.

Triumphant? Power over what and whom?The best resolution is one where you forgive, "forget," and move on, creating a neutral feeling similar to what I was able to do with Amanda and the mean girls. No one should imagine they are carrying 50 lbs. in a backpack. How can you proceed to the mountain top on your journey to success when you're weighed down by the past?

Your Aura Has an Impact on Others

When we overcome being a twit, we are kinder and send out positive energy to the world. When we're a twit, our words or actions can bring out the worst in others. I remember a situation where someone was intentionally mistreating me, and it triggered jealousy in me, which was exactly the person's intention. I got angry and defensive because I was left out of a group activity that I would have enjoyed, and the person knew it. As an adult, I made the mistake of lowering myself to a childish level to match the antagonistic person.

I was unable to act maturely in the heat of the moment. After the text exchange, I decided to eliminate or severely limit interactions with that person and others who bring out the worst in me. I don't like being belittled, teased, or neglected by a so-called friend. I'm also a peacemaker and that invites mistreatment by obnoxious people.

When it comes to friendships that are becoming unpleasant, I prefer avoidance rather than confrontation. For immediate family member situations, I believe avoidance isn't healthy. We have more invested with our spouse and children than we do with friends, acquaintances and coworkers.

When triggered to an extreme level, I sometimes don't act maturely, or in accordance with my values. I no longer want to risk that. From now on, rather than fight, explain, or defend myself, I'd rather take the route of quiet "flight."

How many people have you turned away? Are you aware of such behavior? Do you care?

Pay attention to your feelings and response when someone provokes you. Would you rather contribute unpeaceful energy in the world or participate in peaceful relationships? Act accordingly.

People talk about karma, "what goes around comes around," or getting what you deserve. Happiness results from serving others, living a good moral life, doing the right thing, being productive, and treating others well.

Let it Go

Writing this book has been therapeutic. Taking time away to process my poor treatment of others has brought about embarrassment, thoughts of cringeworthy behavior, sadness that I misspoke or mistreated others, and a resolution to make improvements.

After sharing some of my stories with you, many more incidents come to mind. There could be dozens of people from my past who thought I was an a**hole. I'm trying to clean up my thoughts and language and I know I need to be kind to myself as contemplate and let go of my past offenses.

I'm grateful for the many people in my life who accept me for who I am, who genuinely like me, and who accept me for the mishaps and mistakes I've made and continue to make. I've had to forgive myself, knowing I can't smooth over or make up for my many infractions. What's done is done. What was said was said. I can only move forward.

The healthiest way through the a**hole maze is to let go. Otherwise, you continue to experience emotions which can become resentment. You hang onto it, trap it, and walk around wounded.

It's not healthy to continue analyzing or wishing for things to be different. Every day is a new gift for new experiences and opportunities for us to transform our lives.

9 HOW TO MAKE AMENDS IF YOU'RE AN A**HOLE

The final step forward is personal improvement and reaching some type of closure. Closure might not happen in a tangible way, depending on the situation, and could simply mean accepting your faults without verbal interaction.

Whenever possible, make amends with the person you mistreated. That requires work and overcoming discomfort. Restoring peace to both you and another is optimal.

Awareness

The first step to overcoming your unfavorable ways is to be aware that you're an asshole in the first place. This isn't easy to do in our entitled, indulgent, self-absorbed culture. After awareness comes admission that you're in the wrong.

Sometimes patterns of behavior or ingrained habits block people from recognizing this. For example, if your parents and other people in your life treat people poorly, this might be normal or familiar to you. You might not see a problem. That doesn't mean your behavior is acceptable.

Sometimes others will give you clues as to why it's not okay to mistreat them. You might miss those clues. You need to pay attention to other people's feelings, words, and actions. Observation skills are important. Being exposed to many different personality types is also helpful.

Apology

Showing compassion and telling someone you're sorry is a good start. You then must follow through with acquiring new behaviors and acting kindly. This involves putting the other person first, listening more, seeking to understand another, and avoiding words or actions that might provoke another. An apology is meaningless if there is no remorse, repair, or kindness.

Contemplation and Time Away

If you've offended someone and you've apologized, now is a good time to do some deep thinking about your actions toward the person who thinks you're a twit. You have an opportunity to grow in charity and develop more sensitivity.

Slow your life down a little and take a break from a hectic lifestyle as you consider how you can become a nicer person. When you're constantly busy, you might neglect yourself or authentic connections with others as you rush around completing work and family obligations. Physical exercise, hobbies, and service to others might lift your spirits, especially when a partner or dear friend has created distance and set boundaries.

Accountability

You must face the truth, which means turning your attention to the perception and "truth" the other person has of you. You can get stuck if you focus on your feelings. You can get stuck if you solidify in your mind a story of the incident that has created the distance. You must process the situation from the other person's point of view as best as you can.

Sometimes I don't know why certain friends let me go. I try to guess. Then I avoid doing the things that may have sent them away. With one friend, I talked too much about myself, and she got tired of listening to me. I probably drained or bored her. Maybe she thought of me as a narcissist.

Another friend was sensitive to certain things I said, so I need to exercise more compassion. If I don't take accountability, I might set myself up for the same habits and patterns with others in the future, potentially chasing away new friends – and long-term friends! Even though they might have known us for many years, we shouldn't misbehave with our long-term friends. We still need to treat others impeccably.

Two Possible Pathways

Relationships are good, until they're not. It's odd that things can change in an instant. All it takes is one person to decide they're no longer interested. When Maggie let me go, I didn't know it at the time. It took me a month after making three attempts to communicate with her. She used to reply to me within a short period of time. When there was no response, I figured she was probably done with me.

My friend Didi commented that I had two choices. I could decide that the friendship was probably over and to not reach out again, or I could try to contact her and ask why she didn't return my calls or texts. Didi warned me to be prepared for a response that I might not like. Since I was 90% certain why Maggie no longer wanted to be friends with me, I didn't feel the need to pry.

No one takes pleasure in telling someone why they no longer want to be friends. Many friendships dissolve quietly and gradually. Others may end abruptly and quietly or abruptly and volatile. I can't recall any volatile terminations of my relationships. When endings are imminent, it's best to conclude that the season of your relationship has ended or changed.

When faced with different options, consider the outcomes and purposes of each possibility. My conscience was clear because I gave a heartfelt apology to Maggie on the day she dropped me, so I attempted to repair the relationship. One cannot do further repair when you're not told the offense.

I chose silence because I respected Maggie's intentions to no longer interact with me. I'm learning to be a kinder and gentler person, and I was grateful for Maggie's friendship. The discard resulted in me exploring an unpleasant and rude side of myself, changing my ways to the best of my ability, and writing this book.

Acquiring New Behaviors

Being a twit comes automatic for some people. For occasional twits, unkind actions can be the result of peer pressure or maintaining an image. People also react in mean ways if they've been wronged or if they're protecting or defending something or someone.

Developing emotional maturity, good values and morals, and doing the right thing is the best prevention from being a mean person.

Working on empathy, listening, and selfless action improves the odds that someone won't mistreat others. The reason someone acts unkindly is either they don't care or they're neglectful.

I've noticed that when I want to make a point, I repeat myself. Repetition can be critical or insulting. If I thank a family member for making a nice meal and I offer a suggestion for the next time they make the dish, I don't need to say it two more times in slightly different ways. I should trust that they heard my feedback the first time. Otherwise, it becomes unkind and unhelpful.

A good approach to making improvements and acquiring new behaviors would be to decide that you don't want to be accused of being an asshole. Review Chapter 3, and do the opposite of what was listed in "You Might Be an Asshole If…"

The Platinum Rule

Two qualities to work on are caring and considering the other person's perspective. Have you heard of the "Golden Rule?" The Golden Rule is understood to mean, "Treat others as you want to be treated." Consider the "Platinum Rule" by treating others how they want to be treated, and better than you would like to be treated.

The Platinum Rule involves learning what the other person prefers and how he or she wants to be treated, while the Golden Rule involves guesswork on your part and guesswork related to your preferences.

A tricky issue could be if you're dealing with a person who doesn't feel worthy of good treatment. This is why I believe we need to treat others better than ourselves or better than they want to be treated.

The Platinum Rule involves service and sacrifice which is foreign to twits.

Faith

We must have faith in God, ourselves and nature. Faith in God isn't some desperate, weakness that replaces faith in the self, but rather strengthens a person. Faith in God is the foundation of love. Faith enables us to have compassion for others, to have hope for the future, and is a belief system that aids in a positive life. When we have love for all people, we become aware of how we should treat people.

Faith in ourselves means we know we can change for the better. We seek improvement and expect beneficial outcomes. We trust ourselves and our abilities.

Faith in nature is pivotal in living our daily life. Knowing the basic laws of biology and physics cuts down on frustration. We can see patterns and explanations for various phenomena and occurrences. We can make sound decisions when we understand nature. Learning about the nature of man, in general, is a fascinating topic that explains why we need to eliminate our a**holish ways.

Making amends for your offensive behavior requires awareness, admission, acknowledgement, and apology. If you want to take things to a higher level, acquire new behaviors and adopt the Platinum Rule. Live in accordance with high standards of morality and integrity as you treat other human beings with the utmost respect and compassion.

CONCLUSION

Unless we expose ourselves to ourselves, we will be discontented and disconnected. We won't know what we're striving for and will succumb to frustration, hopelessness, addiction, anxiety, depression and / or despair. We will be riding on a merry-go-round that never stops.

In our brief time together, we've discovered what an a**hole is, why someone treats others poorly, what to do if you are the a**hole or have been a victim, and how to eliminate unkind behavior.

Why You Shouldn't Be an A**hole

Being an a**hole not only exposes the worst in you but has the potential to provoke the worst in others. I'm not proud of myself for surrendering my values in response to those scalawags. I compromised my character, and it didn't feel right at all. I sure hope I'm not guilty of bringing out the worst in others when I act like a scoundrel.

Being an a**hole contributes bad energy in the universe. Bad energy is toxic and contributes to psychological and spiritual pollution. It creates a gloomy cloud and robs people of joy.

Most of us prefer to experience pleasure and joy. We're restless seekers on a quest for love and understanding, peace and happiness.

In that quest, some of us are willing to discover truth, authenticity, and beauty. Others don't want to peel back the onion skin. Most of us don't want to experience discomfort and pain, and some go out of their way to avoid hardship at all costs.

Since I've been at the receiving end of dozens of a**holes and I've acted as one from time to time, I know that those who don't face pain or truth and those who are unsettled tend to feel broken. They have periods of unhappiness and feel as if they're lacking something. They're at risk for causing bad energy in their vicinity.

A**holeness is sometimes a reactionary behavior, and sometimes a proactive intention. I can't think of any collective benefit of being an a**hole or being harmed by one.

Thrive or Survive?

Do you want to thrive or merely survive? Survival mode goes something like this: wake up, go about the business of your day whether that involves work, school, home, or something else. Throw in some errands, other obligations and activities, maybe a little socializing, exercise or hobby. Don't forget grooming, meal preparation, and eating. Rest and repeat the same routine the next day. Non-thrivers are reactive and short-sighted. Fatigue and overwhelm often occur. Sometimes anxiety, worry and depression. Life is a blurring of the days on a conveyor belt or hamster wheel, with occasional adventures and leisure activities.

Thriving means you're energized about big and small goals. You have a mission, or two, or three. You're living your values alongside your passion, being productive and satisfied. You generally love life and feel grateful for how things are going. You have an overall purpose and meaning. Life is fulfilling. You have things to look forward to. You're proactive. You're energetic. You're thriving.

Thrivers can be prone to being unkind if they are steeped in ego and selfishness, but thrivers are often on a path of achievement, accomplishment, and productivity. I think of survivors (as opposed to thrivers) as lost souls, not fully happy with their lives, maybe stuck. They tend to waste their free time on consuming and watching. They're not in the arena in the game of life, but on the sidelines.

Pompous, arrogant thrivers can be a**holes, but many thrivers are busy chasing personal goals and adventures. They aren't concerned with stirring the pot or causing trouble in others' lives. The survivors lack purpose and passion and are more apt to be a**holes, from what I've observed.

A cleaner, more productive world contains people who focus on their mission and passions.

Thrivers generally lead happier, more interesting lives because they are in tune with their gifts, talents, and skills. They have less need to complain, compare, and despair. A person with inner strength and direction doesn't need to bully others.

As they advance in age, the narcissists and a**holes have less friends. No one wants to be around them.

Words Mean Something

I don't like the words asshole, idiot, stupid, and jerk. For unintentional and unaware acts of a**holeness, I prefer softer words like ass, a-hole, "AH," twit, twerp, abrasive, obstinate, obnoxious, unkind, or incorrigible.

For those who are intentional, I would use stronger words and accusations including mean, nasty, malicious, unstable, bear, unbearable, broken, bully, aggressive, narcissist, pompous ass, arrogant, egotistical, or psychopath.

For a full-blown malicious asshole, vulgar words might slip out of my mouth to describe their behavior.

I don't like to call people names or use vulgar words because I don't want to define them. I hope that most people can and will change their objectionable behaviors and treatment of others. As a people pleaser, I don't want to hurt someone's feelings or judge them harshly by using strong language.

I don't feel good when I need to confront someone. I feel like I'm launching a missile in their direction. Words can be hurtful, and a person might imprint words on their soul. If we call someone an a**hole, we put ourselves in a position of authority, as if we know better.

People often react to how they're treated. Can you see how a back-and-forth volley might take place? A person is cruel to someone. The victim responds in a mean manner. The cruel person then escalates the conversation and a destructive interaction ensues.

Peel Back the Onion Skin

A**holes and non-a**holes are worthy of respect. Human dignity. We may not like a**holes, but if we understand them, we might feel sorry for them. Even the ones who are malicious and horrid. Something went wrong somewhere during their development or lifetime.

If we don't uncover what is buried beneath the surface of ourselves, we live in denial. We live in a protective mode, where energy is exerted to keep us safe from admitting and dealing with something that needs to be confronted with and changed.

You could argue that some things are better off remaining buried, but most things must be brought to the surface and addressed. They can then be buried, set aside or forgotten, but we must acknowledge those things about ourselves which cause harm to ourselves and others.

A Community Effort

We don't need this toxic wasteland of unkindness

and lack of compassion. Don't you agree that the world needs less a**holes?

Join the community of recovering and reformed a**holes and share your copy of AITA or give a copy to someone who needs it. I hope you'll agree that this book is a needed resource in how to deal with offensive people and how to avoid being an offensive person.

I'd like to invite you to be an AITA Ambassador by telling at least one other person about this book and posting a review on Amazon. Please share your story with me, at danajbaker123@gmail.com. Instagram: aitadanabaker. Together we can create a more peaceful world.

I want to leave you with one question: What are you building?

PART IV – QUICK LISTS

HOW TO KNOW IF YOU'RE AN A**HOLE

Initially focus on yourself and if you might have said something offensive or acted offensively. Rather than think, "It's not me, it's them," consider the following: "It's not them, it's me." However, don't blame yourself if you're not at fault. This is why it's important to research narcissism and other topics presented in this book.

Ponderings

1. What if I'm the asshole?
2. Have you noticed a difference in how someone treats you or interacts with you? If yes, ask: Have I said or done anything that might be offensive to the person? If so, what, and how do I know?

Nightly Questions

1. Before going to sleep, make a quick review of your day and ask, "Was I an a**hole today to anyone I encountered?
2. What did I say or do today that might have offended or annoyed someone?
3. Did I knowingly provoke someone?
4. Did I make fun of / tease someone today?
5. Did I say hurtful or negative comments to anyone?

You Might Be an A**hole If...

1. You intrude, meddle, and interrupt frequently.
2. You don't help others but instead sabotage them or perform practical jokes that can be interpreted as mean.
3. You purposely say and do things to irritate someone.
4. You lie, cheat, and steal.
5. You're disrespectful and condescending.
6. Your dog doesn't like you and runs away from you.
7. Your children and relatives don't like being in your presence and avoid you.
8. You have narcissistic tendencies.
9. You protect your ego or image at all costs.
10. You've been called an asshole.

HOW TO AVOID BEING AN
A**HOLE

Behavioral Tips

1. Be a producer, not a consumer. Make your life worthwhile, not problematic.
2. Give more than you take.
3. THINK before you speak (True, Helpful, Inspiring, Needed, Kind).
4. Follow non-violent communication (Observation, Feeling, Need, Request).
5. Be a truth-seeker. Make it your mission to develop a realistic view of yourself, others, and the world.
6. Follow the Platinum Rule: Treat others better than you want to be treated and how they want to be treated.
7. Don't show up late and make others wait. In

other words, don't always put yourself first or at the center of the universe.

8. Be kind, thoughtful, and helpful.
9. Respect other people's boundaries.
10. Don't gossip or slander.
11. Make a list with 2 columns: Problem and Remedy. Use "I" statements. Example: Problem: I interrupt too much. Remedy: I will wait to speak.

Psychological Tips

1. Be grateful for everything you have and everything you are.
2. Don't compete, and instead, create. Create something in accordance with your interests, skills and talents.
3. Don't compare, or you'll despair. You are not less than anyone. Start believing you are here on Earth to make unique contributions to benefit mankind. Act accordingly.
4. Your identity is not held hostage to your childhood. Break free or at least find new coping mechanisms. Overcome obstacles and find new strategies.
5. Get out of your head, get busy with meaningful endeavors, and help others.
6. Check your ego at the door. Overinflated egos invite arrogance, condescension, narcissism, and lack of empathy and compassion. Figure out how to integrate heathy ego and pride.
7. Be comfortable with your own ignorance.
8. Embrace vulnerability, loneliness, and being

comfortable with yourself.
9. Live a virtuous life.
10. Avoid jealousy, envy, comparing, and in many cases competing.
11. Love others.

HOW TO DEAL WITH AN A**HOLE

There are a variety of ways you can interact with a twit. It depends on how severely you've been violated, and if you have obligations to others who are twits.

1. Keep your distance.
2. Maintain minimal contact.
3. Use non-violent communication.
4. Avoid the person entirely.
5. Be quiet. Be quiet in their presence and outside their presence. You may warn others but be aware that your dynamic with them is different. Don't get entangled in gossip, defamation or slander.
6. Respond assertively. Protect and defend yourself firmly.

7. Gently guide them to a better way of behaving. A**holes don't like to be corrected, directed, or criticized, so tread carefully and offer a solution or technique, not empty or threatening words.

8. Educate yourself. Change your ways of interacting with the person. Don't compromise your character. Make adjustments, especially if your boss or a close family member is a twit.

9. Be polite and say hello. Keep conversations neutral and minimal.

10. Pray for them. Pray for yourself.

11. Forgive them. Forgive yourself. No blame. If blame, no gain.

12. Take some time to reflect.

13. Form a coalition. Have higher expectations of the offender. Sometimes higher expectations lead to better relationships and results.

14. Be counterintuitive. Invite the bully to join your club or team. Ask the person to participate, which is offering him or her a chance to make a meaningful contribution. The outsider might shift his or her attitude and transform their behavior. However, beware of the person who is a saboteur. Give them only one chance and carefully monitor them.

15. Stand up for yourself. Keep boundaries strong and firm.

16. Seek counseling from a skilled professional.

MYTHS AND UNTRUTHS ABOUT A**HOLES

1. You can out clever an a**hole.

   No. Don't get entangled. The situation might escalate to something you don't want.

2. Revenge is the best tactic when you've been wronged. Witnessing karma would be sweet.

   No. Don't take the bait or get trapped. You have no way of knowing how things will turn out if you lower yourself to the level of the twit.

3. A**holes know when they're wrong.

   No. Not all the time. Some acts are intentional, and some aren't.

4. A**holes are all the same.

    No. A**holes are not created equal. Some are opportunists. Some are chronic. Others are tempted occasionally. Some are reactionary. Some seem downright evil. The level of a**holeness varies. Some incidences are mild and relatively easy to recover from. Other actions are unbearable.

5. A**holes are less likely than their victims to remember their harmful shenanigans.

    Not true. We all have consciences. People don't admit shameful incidents from their past and present. It's painful. Some people are haunted for many years by what they did to others.

ABOUT THE AUTHOR

Dana Baker, author of *Cult Deception: How a Personal Development Company Seduced Me and How I Broke Free* and *Am I the A**hole?: Your Words and Actions Matter*, is a cult survivor, veteran, and former human resources (HR) manager who knows the good, the bad, and the ugly about human relationships. Many people avoid "the elephant in the room," but she tackles the taboo. Dana believes if we don't shed light on issues that need to be discussed, they'll fester in the dark.

Other books by Dana Baker

Cult Deception: How a Personal Development Company Seduced Me and How I Broke Free

In this riveting true story, Dana Baker describes her innocent entry into what she thought was a self-improvement organization to her abrupt exit from what was a harmful, mind-boggling institution. The moment Dana enters "Duped Development," readers will be intrigued with her story, and will be surprised at the prevalence of mind control and group hypnosis all around us.
Readers will learn the dangers of cults and how to avoid being deceived by lofty promises. The most educated and emotionally strong among us can be susceptible to brainwashing.